THE HEALTHY HABITS
HANDBOOK

THE HEALTHY HABITS

HANDBOOK

BY

SLIM GOODBODY

PHOTOGRAPHS BY BRUCE CURTIS
ILLUSTRATIONS BY NURIT KARLIN

COWARD-McCANN, INC.   NEW YORK

Costume © 1974 John Burstein
Text copyright © 1983 by John Burstein
Illustrations copyright © 1983 by Nurit Karlin
Photographs copyright © 1983 by Bruce Curtis
Initial Research by Mary Ellen Rohon
Published simultaneously
in Canada by General Publishing Co. Limited, Toronto.
First printing
Printed in the United States of America
Costume constructed at Ray Diffen Stage
Clothes, Inc., New York

Library of Congress Cataloging in Publication Data
Burstein, John.
The healthy habits handbook.
Includes index
Summary: Explains and demonstrates good health
habits, emphasizing the individual's responsibility to
make wise choices about what to wear, how much to
exercise, and how to spend free time.
1. Health—Juvenile literature. [1. Health]
I. Karlin, Nurit, ill. II. Curtis, Bruce, ill.
III. Title.
RA777.B858   1983   613   83-7597
ISBN 0-698-20590-1
ISBN 0-698-20592-8 (pbk.)

CONTENTS

This book is all about healthy habits.
Doing good things for yourself everyday.
Becoming your own best friend.

The truth is: Good health is up to you. Your parents, teachers and doctor can offer advice and make suggestions, but *you* have to follow through. Each day you are faced with choices to make about how you treat yourself—what kinds of foods you put into your body, how much exercise to give your muscles, how to spend your free time, and so on. Each choice provides you with an opportunity to increase your fitness. Healthy living is an exciting challenge.

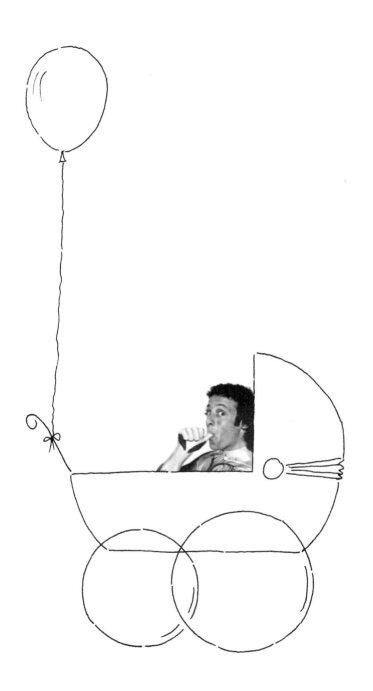

INTRODUCTION

When you were a little baby, people took care of you. They chose what food you ate, when you bathed, how you dressed, when you went outside and made almost every other decision you could think of. But now that you've grown older, more and more things are left up to you. Your parents, who were once the rulers of your life, have changed positions and become your guides. They now point the way but don't force you to follow it. You may be wondering if this is true, so think about this example.

Your mother tells you that you have to brush your teeth after breakfast. Let's even say that she makes it an order. You go into the bathroom to obey, but once the door is closed, she doesn't really know what you're doing. You could just run the water and pretend to be brushing. Nobody really knows but you.

And you're the only one who truly benefits or suffers by your actions.

When you practice healthy habits you're doing it FOR YOURSELF! You'll be living in and with your body for the rest of your life, and it's your responsibility to make it a strong and happy home. The way you treat yourself now will affect you in the future.

I'll be explaining and demonstrating most of the important things that need to be done in order for you to be healthy. I hope you learn and grow and become the best you can be.

DAILY HEALTHY HABITS

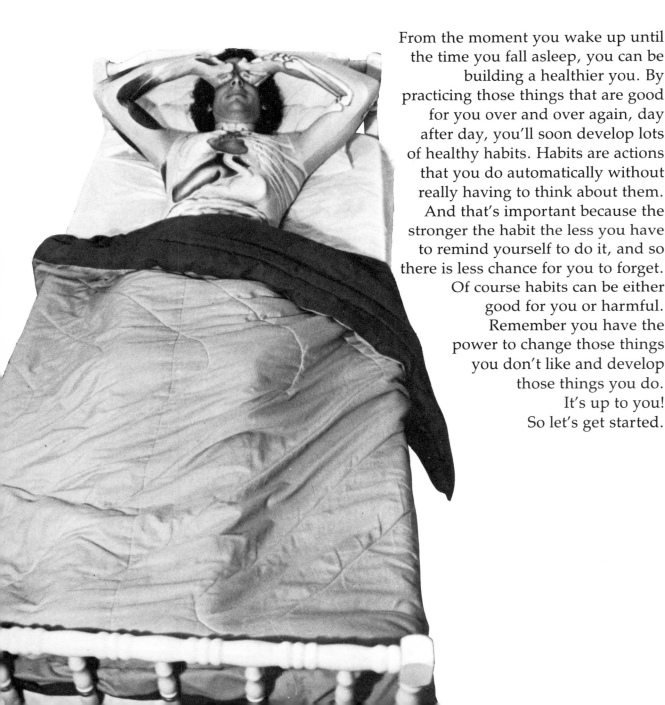

From the moment you wake up until the time you fall asleep, you can be building a healthier you. By practicing those things that are good for you over and over again, day after day, you'll soon develop lots of healthy habits. Habits are actions that you do automatically without really having to think about them. And that's important because the stronger the habit the less you have to remind yourself to do it, and so there is less chance for you to forget. Of course habits can be either good for you or harmful. Remember you have the power to change those things you don't like and develop those things you do. It's up to you! So let's get started.

HELLO, DAY

When you first wake up in the morning, it's a good idea to take a few moments to prepare yourself for the start of new day. While still in bed you can do a few simple stretches for your body. These will get your muscles moving and your blood circulating.

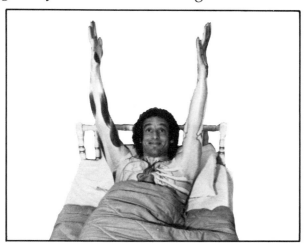

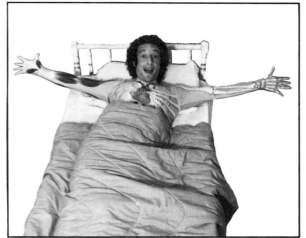

And to prepare yourself mentally, say a few simple phrases softly or silently. Some suggestions are:

1. Something good is going to happen today.

2. Today is the first day of the rest of my life.

3. Today is unknown territory, and I am a brave explorer making my way through it.

4. Every day in every way, I'm getting better and better.

5. I'll be good to my body today.

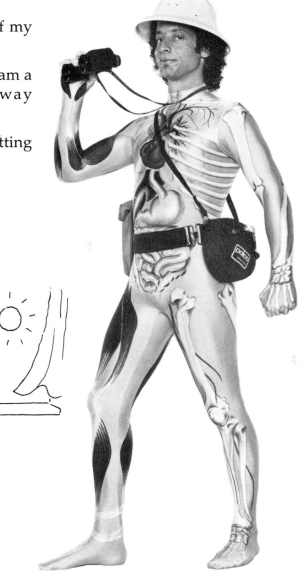

SUIT YOURSELF

The clothes you choose to wear are important to your physical and mental health. When deciding what to wear, be guided by the weather and by your plans for the day.

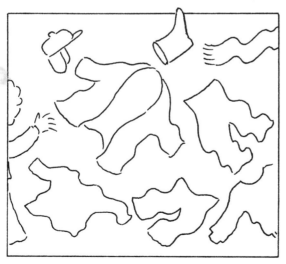

If it is cold out:

1. Dress in layers because:

   a) The layers keep a small cushion of air between them, and this insulation helps keep you warm.

   b) When you go inside where it's warm, you can take off one or more layers (such as a sweater) until you're feeling comfortable.

2. Wear a hat. A great deal of your body's heat is lost through the top of your head.

If it is warm out:

1. Wear light-colored clothes. They reflect the rays of the sun.

2. Bring a sweater or jacket along to any place there might be air conditioning.

3. Be sure your clothes are comfortable and loose fitting.

RECHARGING YOUR BODY BATTERIES

After a good night's sleep, your body needs a fresh fuel supply to keep it running strong throughout the morning. That's why breakfast is so important. You are *breaking* (ending) your *fast* (the time you don't eat). Many people forget that even while they sleep, their bodies are busy at work. The heart is beating, blood is flowing, lungs are breathing, muscles are moving, and your brain is dreaming. All these tasks take energy. The energy is provided by last night's dinner, but by the time the morning rolls around it's used up. Breakfast provides a fresh supply. Studies have shown that children who eat a good morning meal are more alert and do better in school. Here are foods you should include:

CHOMP, CHOMP, CHEW, CHEW, CHEW

Of course your teeth are important when you smile because they make your face so friendly and nice. But their main job is chewing, and it's essential to your health that you let them do their work well. The truth is, digestion begins in your mouth, not your stomach. Chewing breaks food down into small enough pieces to be safely swallowed, and the saliva that gets mixed in during the process starts dissolving the food chemically. By gobbling your food down, you're not getting the most out of what you eat, and your stomach has to work harder.

Different teeth do different jobs—

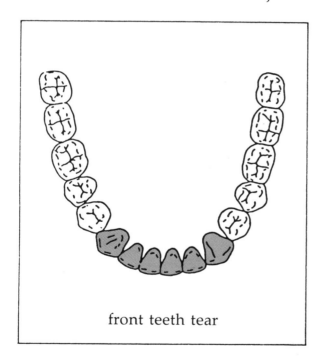

front teeth tear

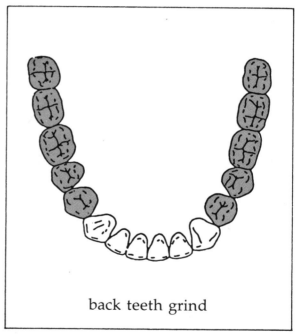

back teeth grind

Be sure all the food you eat is wet and soft before letting it leave the mouth and continue on its journey.

GREET YOUR TEETH

After breakfast, go to the bathroom and get ready to clean those hardworking teeth. But first, smile and say "Thanks teeth!" Now begin to take good care of them by brushing and flossing.

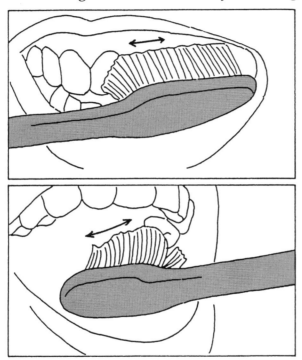

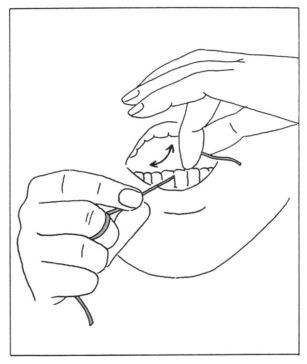

Cavities get started when food gets left behind in your mouth after you eat. It's been proven that with proper dental care you will hardly ever get a cavity. Brushing cleans the surface of the tooth, and flossing gets into those tight places a brush can't reach.

Did you know that almost 90 percent of cavities form between the teeth? That's why it's so important to get in there with floss at least once a day.

HUG AND AWAY

When it's time to leave home, share a moment of love with mom, dad or a loved one. Just as breakfast recharged your body batteries, a hug will plug a love current into your heart. Now you can go through the day feeling warm inside. Before you go, check out the time you'll be seeing each other again.

And you're on your way!

SCHOOL DAYS

Going to school is a real adventure. There is so much to learn and so many things to share. Just think, almost one-half of your waking hours are spent in school, so try to get the most out of the experience.

School will help you develop your mind and body and teach you about working with others. These are all elements of a healthy life.

SIT STRAIGHT

Classroom posture is very important. After sitting in your seat for a long time, your body can feel tense and your muscles cramped. When you learn to sit in the correct way and to use your muscles as they were supposed to be used, you'll be able to stay much more alert and feel more comfortable.

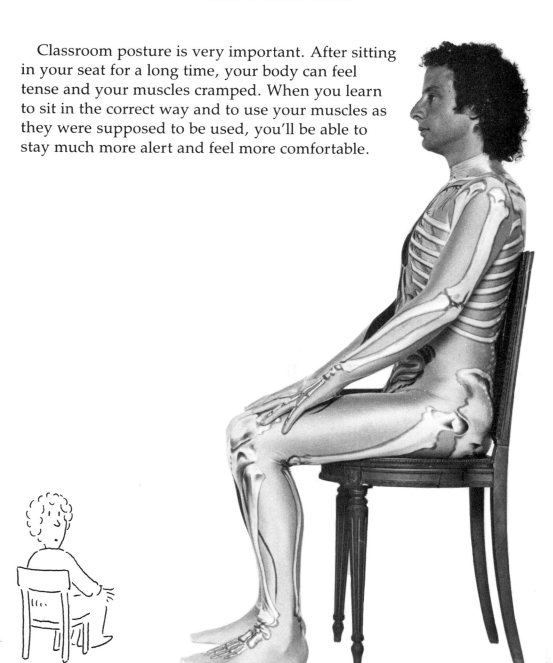

When you read a book at your desk, raise the book to eye level instead of bending forward to read. Your head weighs several pounds, and by hanging it over, you're straining neck and shoulder muscles.

When writing, practice good posture as well.

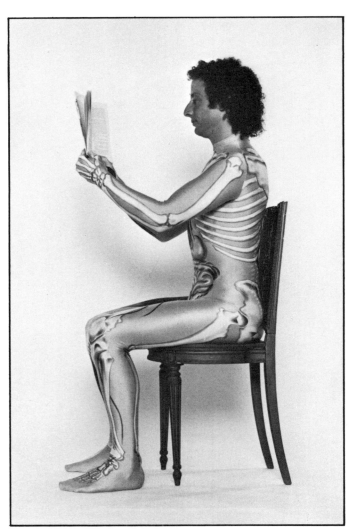 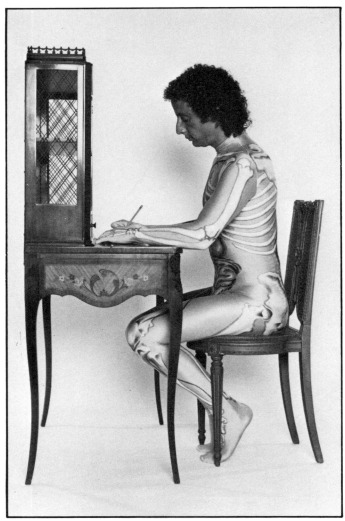

SCHOOL SAFETY

Many accidents can happen during school hours, but most are easy to avoid! The key to being safe is being *aware*. By paying attention to what you're doing throughout the day, you won't get careless and so you won't get hurt. Here are some school safety tips to follow:

INSIDE

1. Obey safety rules.

2. *Walk* on stairs and in the hall.

3. Remain calm and orderly during fire drills.

4. See the nurse if you feel sick or hurt yourself.

1. Keep a good distance away from people using the swings.

2. Always warn your partner when you're getting off the seesaw or chaning the rules of a game.

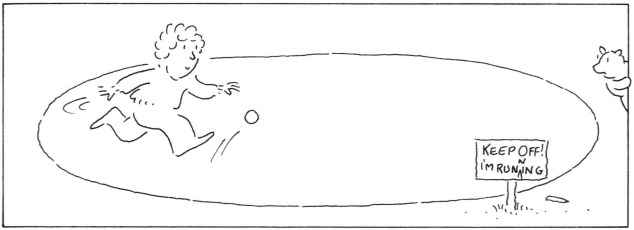

3. Never run with a stick or pointed object in your hand.

4. Give yourself plenty of space when playing running games.

If you follow my advice, it will help you have a healthy school year.

LUNCH TIME / MUNCH TIME

Whether you bring food from home or get it at school, be sure to eat your lunch. Even though you may not realize it, the school day takes a lot of energy out of you. Did you know that a lot of the power we get from food is used by our brains? And while you're in school, your brain is kept very busy. Lunchtime is the right time to stock up with a fresh fuel supply.

There are lots of different foods to eat that are good for you. Sometimes it's fun to share.

When you're sitting with your friends and everyone is talking and having a good time, you may forget to chew your food slowly and well. Try to remember to go slow and not gobble your food down.

When you're finished eating take a few moments to relax and let your body begin digesting the food. Then go on and enjoy yourself.

HAPPY FACE

Smiling is contagious. Spread it around. As you go through the day, a nice smile can send a beam of human sunshine to the people you meet. They'll feel good and probably flash back a grin, which will brighten up your day.

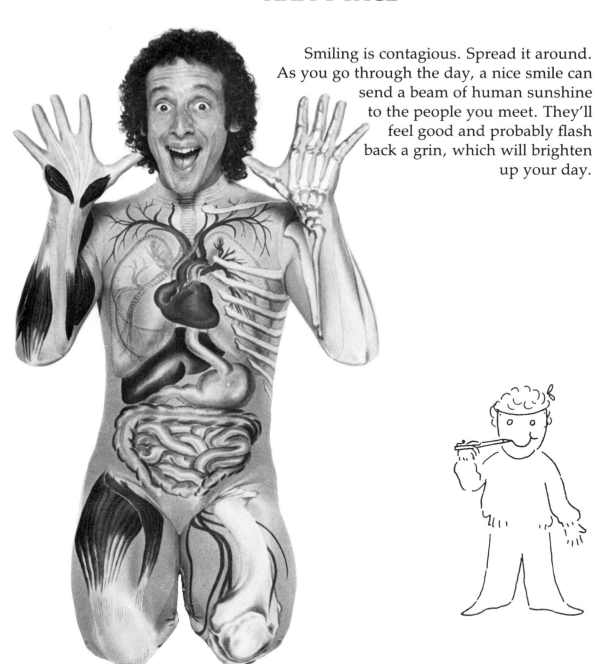

UNHAPPY FACE

Smiling is great, but if you are feeling
really unhappy, it's very important not
to hide it behind a grin. Covering up
feelings doesn't get rid of them, they still
stay inside, ready to come out. It's best to
talk about the things that upset you with
someone you trust. This way you can let
off some steam and discover ways of
making yourself feel better. Sharing feelings
is a very important healthy habit.

PRESSURE COOKER

There are certain times in school (and elsewhere) when you feel a lot of pressure. Often it happens when you are being tested or asked a question. Maybe you're trying out for a team or a part in a play. Your muscles get tight and your body feels tense. Now is the time to do a few relaxation exercises:

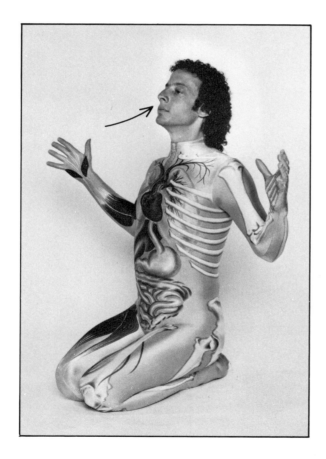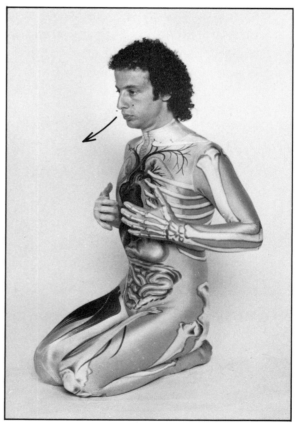

1. Take three deep breaths in through your nose. Inhale and exhale slowly.

2. Tense up all your muscles for a moment and then relax them.

3. Count down backwards from 10 and tell yourself that you're growing calmer and calmer.

4. Concentrate for a moment on something pleasant that has recently happened or that you hope will happen soon.

5. When you've only got a few seconds to relax, take a quick breath in and, as you let it out, silently say, "Relax."

Of course, it's best to be prepared for situations that can make you feel tense.

WARM-UPS

If you're going to get involved in vigorous exercise, be sure that your muscles are warmed-up well before you begin. By taking a few moments out to stretch and loosen, you'll be protecting yourself from many possible injuries.

Here are some warm-ups you can do:

1. Stretching hamstrings

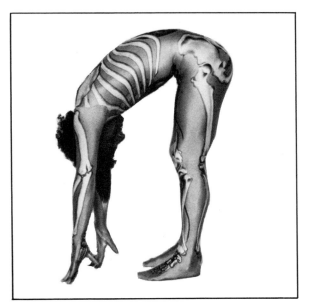

2. Bending over

3. Jumping up and down

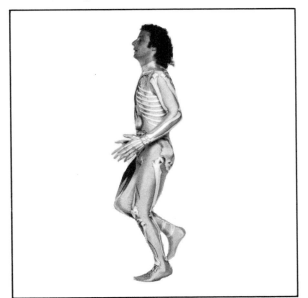

4. Running in place

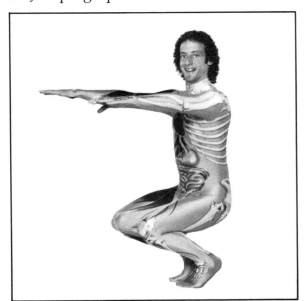

5. Deep knee bends

YOUR TIME

When school is over and planned activities are through, you have the chance to spend some exciting time with a very special person: You. This is a time to explore new things, develop new talents and learn more about yourself. It's a time to meet the qualities that make up You, to find out what you like about yourself and what you may want to change. There are so many things you can do:

1. Listen to music or play an instrument

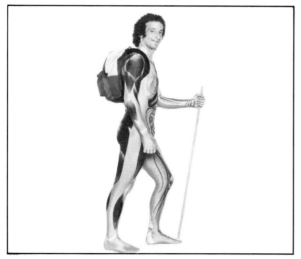

2. Take a hike

3. Read a book

4. Build a model

5. Daydream

We spend so much time with other people that we sometimes forget how to be alone. Part of a healthy life is to enjoy the quiet times you spend with yourself.

SHARED TIME

Friendship is an essential ingredient in healthy, happy living. We all need other people. We depend upon them for love, companionship, support and advice. Being a good friend isn't always easy. It takes time, energy and effort. It means knowing a lot about other people and their likes, dislikes, moods, beliefs and abilities. Discovering all of this information takes time and patience—but it's worth it!

Here are some things you can do to practice being a good friend:

1. Listen carefully to your friend.

2. If something is told to you in confidence, keep it to yourself.

3. Be honest.

4. Share your feelings and thoughts.

5. Be generous with praise, but know how to give constructive criticism.

6. Try not to embarrass your friend in front of others.

The rewards of friendship are sharing, loving and giving.

SNACKING

Your muscles make energy from the food you eat to work and play. Sometimes three meals just aren't enough to get you through the day. When your power supply is weak, snacking gives you that extra boost of energy to get back into action. Be sure to eat a wholesome snack. Candy and soda, which have lots of sugar, will give you quick energy but it only lasts a few minutes. Then your body is more tired than before. When choosing a snack, try to pick a food that is natural and healthy. A piece of fruit, cheese, peanut butter, carrots, nuts and seeds are all good. If you eat something from a jar, can or box, read the label to see what ingredients it contains. This will let you know whether or not you're filling up on a product high in sugar that will let you down in a short while.

CONTENTS OF SOFT DRINK

CARBONATED WATER,

SUGAR,

CARAMEL COLOR,

PHOSPHORIC ACID,

NATURAL FLAVORINGS,

CAFFEINE.

Label reading. The item listed first is the one that occurs in the largest quantity in the product.

DINNER WINNER

When you reach the last meal of the day, be sure you wind up a nutritional winner. Think back to everything you've eaten all day long to see if you've eaten a wide variety of wholesome foods. An easy guide to good nutrition is making sure you've eaten a lot of different-colored foods throughout the day. For example: red tomatoes, yellow corn, white-meat chicken, purple grapes, green lettuce, and so on. Often dinner is the time you get to eat most of your vegetables. Vegetables contain many of the vitamins and minerals necessary for good health. If you review your day's meals and discover that you haven't eaten any, then be sure to get your share at dinner.

Dinnertime is a good time to share ideas and feelings with loved ones.

Did you drink enough fluids today? We all need from six to eight glasses a day to stay healthy!

FOOD GROUP	RECOMMENDED DAILY SERVINGS	ALTERNATE SOURCES	NUTRIENT SUPPLIED
Size of Serving *MILK* 1 cup milk or yogurt	3	1½ slices (1½ oz) cheddar cheese* 1 cup pudding 1¾ cups ice cream 2 cups cottage cheese*	Calcium Riboflavin (B₂) Protein
MEAT 2 ounces lean, cooked meat, fish or poultry	2	2 eggs 2 slices (2 oz.) cheddar cheese* ½ cup cottage cheese* 1 cup dried beans or peas 4 tablespoons peanut butter	Protein Niacin Iron Thiamin (B₁)
FRUIT-VEGETABLE ½ cup cooked vegetable or juice 1 cup raw (medium sized piece of fruit)	4		Vitamin A (retinol) Vitamin C (ascorbic acid)
GRAIN (whole grain, fortified and enriched) 1 slice bread 1 cup ready-to-eat cereal ½ cup cooked cereal, pasta or grits	4		Carbohydrate Thiamin (B₁) Niacin Iron

*Cheese should be counted as *either* a serving of milk OR meat, but not *both*.

NUTRIENT	FOOD SOURCES	WHAT IT DOES FOR THE BODY
PROTEIN	meat, poultry, fish, dried beans and peas, eggs, cheese, milk	It is part of every body cell and helps them grow strong.
CARBOHYDRATE	cereal, potatoes, dried beans, corn, bread, sugar	Helps grow new body cells and keep them healthy. In unrefined form, they provide fiber.
FAT	shortening, oil, butter, margarine, salad dressing, sausages	Fats are part of every body cell. They supply fatty acids the body needs. Gives the body vitamins A, D, E & K, which are fat soluble.
VITAMIN A (retinol)	liver, carrots, sweet potatoes, greens, butter, margarine	Helps in the formation of skin and mucous membranes in body cavities, such as the nose and intestines. Helps us to have healthy eyes.
VITAMIN C (ascorbic acid)	broccoli, orange, grapefruit, papaya, mango, strawberries	Makes collagen, which holds the body's cells together, strengthens blood vessels and helps in the healing of bones and cuts. Also helps the body use iron.
THIAMIN (B_1)	lean pork, nuts, fortified cereals	Helps the body use carbohydrates; gives you a normal appetite; helps the nervous system work properly.
RIBOFLAVIN (B_2)	liver, milk, yogurt, cottage cheese	Works as an enzyme to make energy in the body's cells; gives the body healthy skin, eyes and clear vision.
NIACIN	liver, meat, poultry, fish, peanuts, fortified cereals	Aids the body in the use of fats and carbohydrates; helps the body's tissues breathe; promotes healthy skin, nerves and digestion.
CALCIUM	milk, yogurt, cheese, sardines and salmon with bones, collard, kale and turnip greens	Strengthens teeth and bones; helps in blood clotting; aids in normal muscle contraction and relaxation and helps messages travel through the nerves.
IRON	enriched farina, prune juice, liver, dried beans and peas, red meat	Iron and protein combine to make hemoglobin, the red part of blood that takes oxygen *to* and carbon dioxide *from* the cells; prevents anemia and fatigue; helps the body fight infections.

WORK AT HOME

School helps you develop your mind in many ways. Not only are you taught to read, write and reason, but you also have to take responsibility for knowing your lessons. Homework is often hard work, but it does help make you mentally stronger and more disciplined. The important thing to remember when it's time to sit down and begin your homework is that you are not doing it for your teacher, you are doing it for yourself. What you learn becomes your own mental property. Information is a tool that will help you get along in life. Taking responsibility for a task and mastering it are very important parts in the process of growing up.

When doing your homework:

1. Choose a quiet place.

2. Make sure the light is good.

3. Begin early before you're too tired to think clearly.

4. Take frequent breaks to rest your eyes and stretch your muscles.

5. Ask your parents to help you if you don't understand the assignment.

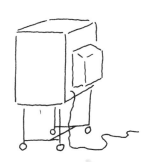

SAFE AT HOME

While you're home, be aware that there are dangers to be avoided. Many of the household objects we depend upon can cause accidents if we don't use them properly. Be alert to household dangers and help prevent them. Remember safety habits are healthy habits!

To stay safe:

FROM FALLS:

1. Put toys and games away after playing. Don't leave them on floor or stairs.

2. Wipe spilled liquids up right away.

3. Use a sturdy ladder to reach things high up.

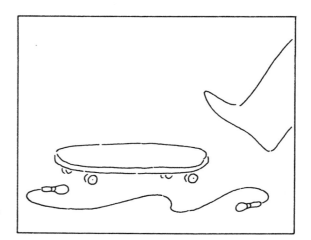

FROM ELECTRICAL SHOCKS

1. Keep hands and body dry whenever you touch an electrical appliance.

2. Grip the plug when you pull it out. Don't yank it by the wire.

FROM SCALDS AND BURNS

1. Turn handles of pots and pans inward on the stove.

2. Stand clear of a frying pan with hot grease in it.

3. Use a potholder to handle a hot object.

4. Dip your hand into bath water before stepping in.

5. Keep cloth or paper off a hot stove.

FROM POISONING

1. Never put anything into your mouth unless you are 100 percent certain it's safe.

2. If food looks or smells strange, don't eat it.

3. Never take medicine unless a trusted adult gives it to you.

WATCH IT!

Too much television is not a good idea. It can be a way of wasting time. That isn't to say that there aren't worthwhile programs. Of course there are. But too often, once people sit down in front of the tube, they become almost hypnotised and watch program after program without really realizing it.

Life is full of opportunities to do things, and spending hours watching television takes up a lot of valuable time that could be used developing other interests.

When watching television:

1. Don't sit too close.

2. Decide on the amount of time you'll spend watching before you start. Then stick to it.

3. Think about what you're watching. Not everything you see and hear is true.

4. You might want to talk about the program with a family member.

KEEP IT CLEAN

Skin is an envelop that you wash with soap. It's your outside hide that keeps your fluids inside. And it needs to be kept clean. Dirt and germs get caught in the folds and wrinkles of your skin and are trapped there by your skin's natural oils. Washing removes them.

For a tingling, glowing, healthy body:

1. Wash your hands before eating.

2. Wash your hands after going to the bathroom.

3. Shower or take a bath as often as necessary—at least once every other day.

4. Lather up with your favorite mild soap and scrub away the oil that traps the dirt.

Of course it's important to keep your hair clean as well, so shampoo your hair whenever it starts feeling oily or dirty. Brush or comb it well afterward.

GOOD NIGHT

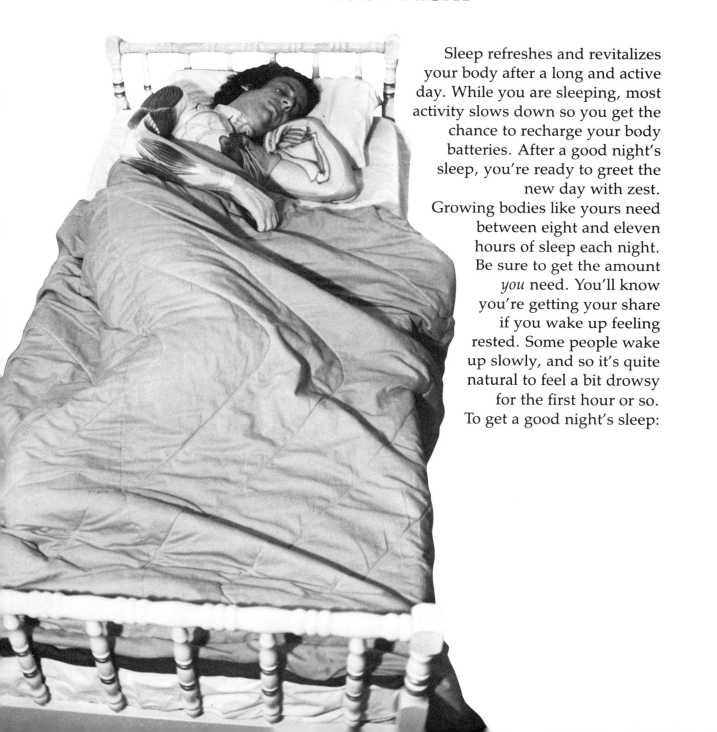

Sleep refreshes and revitalizes your body after a long and active day. While you are sleeping, most activity slows down so you get the chance to recharge your body batteries. After a good night's sleep, you're ready to greet the new day with zest. Growing bodies like yours need between eight and eleven hours of sleep each night. Be sure to get the amount *you* need. You'll know you're getting your share if you wake up feeling rested. Some people wake up slowly, and so it's quite natural to feel a bit drowsy for the first hour or so. To get a good night's sleep:

1. Spend some quiet time before settling down for the night. Reading a book or spending time with mom or dad is a good idea.

2. Wear clean and comfortable night clothes—warm and cozy in winter; cool and loose-fitting in summer.

3. Let a little fresh air circulate through your bedroom if possible. You can do this by opening the window a bit at top and bottom.

4. Think back over the good things that happened to you today and imagine the nice things you'll do tomorrow.

YOUR WHEEL OF HEALTH

Imagine for a moment that healthy living is like a wheel. All the spokes represent different healthy habits. When they are all strong and solid, the wheel can roll freely and easily—provided, of course, that the central hub is firmly in place. That hub is self-love: a sense of deep pride and self-respect. Your body is amazing. It's full of wonders—and that makes you amazing and wonderful. There is nobody exactly like you in the whole world, and that makes you special.

When you understand this and truly love yourself, you'll do everything in your power to give yourself the very best of care. Because you deserve it.

Anything we love, we take care of. A baseball glove, a doll, a favorite toy. Well, just think about your body. It is the most important possession you'll ever have. Love it. Care for it. And become the best you can be.

INDEX